The Best NEW ORLEANS COOKBOOK

Authentic Cajun and Creole recipes from NOLA

Francois Pierre

THE BEST NEW ORLEANS COOKBOOK

CAJUN & CREOLE RECIPES FROM NEW ORLEANS

By
Savour Press
Copyright © by Wentworth Publishing House
All rights reserved

Published by
Savour Press, a DBA of Wentworth Publishing House

Let's get it started!

Welcome to Savour. Have you tried eating Cajun and Creole dishes? Well, these cuisines have one origin and that is Louisiana, known as the place of the Big Easy. Louisianans are proud of what their ancestors have contributed to the world, such as the famous Cajun and Creole cuisines. Although the food presentation is almost similar, they differentiate in some respects, and that is what this book all about. We present to you our best Creole and Cajun recipes that will truly leave your tongue drooling. Our recipes cover a variety of meals, such as stews, soups & side dishes, bread & breakfast, appetizers & salad, sauce & marinades, and main courses. Some of the most popular NOLA dishes are jambalaya, gumbos, Étouffée, and some popular recipes with a touch of Cajun and Creole, such as kebabs, BBQ, fried catfish, sliders, and a lot more. It's the Cajun seasoning, and the blending of celery, onion, garlic, and bell peppers that gives magical touch to make the dishes authentic. As you go through the pages of this book, you will discover how the different jambalaya and gumbo recipes are given a twist of Creole and Cajun.

About This Book

We've been discovering more dishes as we gain knowledge in reading cookbooks, blogs, and watch food vlogs. One of the cuisines that are so popular is Creole and Cajun. But how does each cuisine differ? A simple way of differentiating them is that Creole is known as the city food and Cajun as a country food. Why is this so? The cooking styles and ingredients may vary and blame it on the people behind them. Where to find authentic Creole and Cajun dishes in Louisiana, is to look for homes where they came from, and that is from the neighborhoods scattered all over the state. Although they have distinct cultures and traditions, both Cajun and Creole keep evolving and blending despite their different origins. Creole is an amalgam of cultural influences of Spanish, French, West African, and Amerindian including Southern United States cuisine. In short, Creole is considered aristocratic or elite compared to Cajun, but generally both cuisines are delicious, even if it's your first time to taste them. Let's get ready to have a fun time!

Copyright © 2021 by Savour Press

All rights reserved. No part of this publication may be reproduced, distributed, or transmitted in any form or by any means, including photocopying, recording, or other electronic or mechanical methods, without the prior written permission of the publisher, except in the case of brief quotations embodied in critical reviews and certain other noncommercial uses permitted by copyright law.

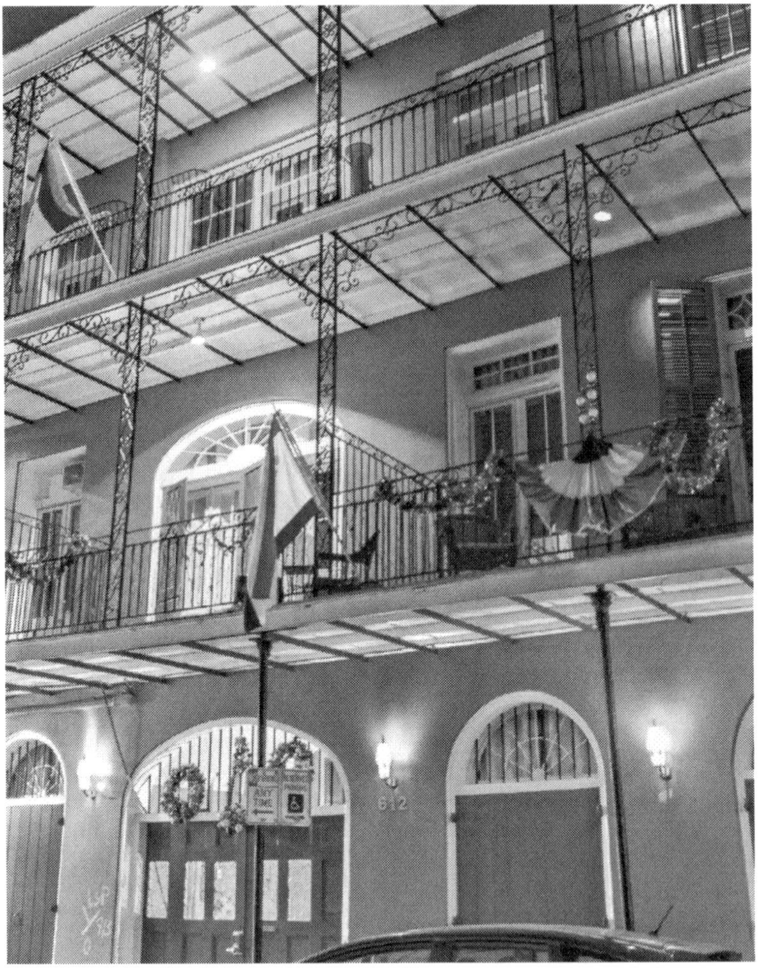
612

TABLE OF CONTENTS

Introduction
Classic Shrimp Creole
Cheesy Shrimp and Grits
Easy Shrimp & Sausage Gumbo
Best-Ever Shrimp Étouffée
New Orleans Gumbo with Shrimp and Sausage
Best-Ever Fried Catfish
Easy Cajun Jambalaya
Cajun Chicken
Cajun BBQ Chicken
Cajun Parmesan Salmon
Cajun Shrimp with Bell Peppers & Corn
Cajun Shrimp Kebabs
Cajun Rice Bake
New Orleans BBQ Shrimp
Red Beans and Rice with Ground Beef
Slow-Cooker Jambalaya
Shrimp Po'Boy Sliders
Easy Beignets
Louisiana Shrimp Dip
Cajun Chicken Sausage Alfredo
Creole Potato Salad
Cajun Spice
Thibodeaux Gumbo
Cajun Pasta
Cajun Turkey
Louisiana Boudin
Cajun Prawns
Savour Press's Classical Creole Chicken
Baton Rouge Gravy
Creole Cake
Creole Meatloaf

Crawfish and Shrimp
Cajun Burger
Cajun Breakfast
Cajun Bisque
Jambalaya
Creole Corn
Creole Fried Snapper
Creole Fried Catfish
Cajun fries
New Orleans Barbecue Shrimp
Po'Boy
Bourbon Chicken
Louisiana Popcorn
Cajun Country Dough
Okra Creole
Conclusion

INTRODUCTION

Which is better Creole or Cajun? If you have tasted both cuisines, you really can't say that one is way better than the other as they are delicious, savory and flavorful. Although Creole dishes are loaded with exotic ingredients and a wide variety of cultures infused into their cooking, you can't say that Cajun is way behind. For example, tomatoes are visible in a Creole Jambalaya while a Cajun Jambalaya does not have nor shall we say a roux in a Cajun recipe is a mixture of flour and oil, while roux in Creole recipe is made of flour and butter. So, if you find this intriguing, it is about time to see the 21 Creole and Cajun recipes that we share in this cookbook. Let's not make an issue about which one is better than the other, as they are both satisfying to your palate, easy to prepare and healthy as well.

Enjoy!

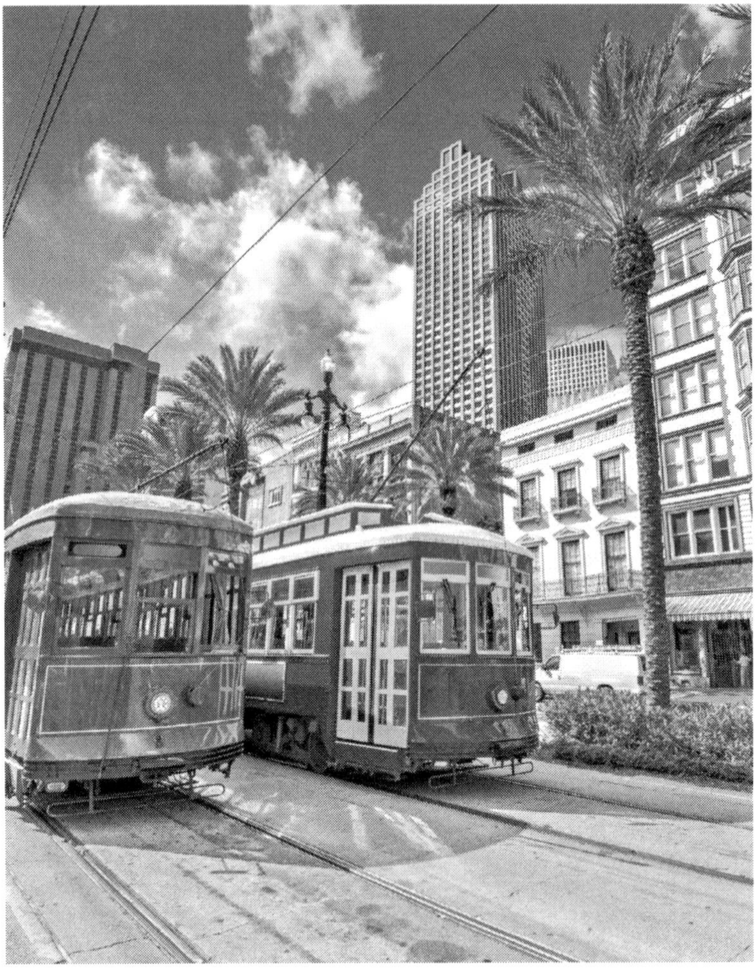

Soups, Stew & Side Dishes

Classic Shrimp Creole

Feel the ambiance of New Orleans by prepping this better version of Shrimp Creole. The tail-on shrimp is drenched in tomato-based sauce with zesty flavor. If you dislike spicy shrimp, just lessen the amount of cayenne.

Servings: 6

Ingredients

3 tablespoons **butter**

1 chopped **green bell pepper**

1 chopped small **onion**

2 chopped **ribs celery**

Freshly ground **black pepper**

Kosher salt

4 minced **cloves garlic**

2 teaspoons **dried thyme**

1 tablespoon **paprika**

1 teaspoon **cayenne**

2 teaspoons **dried oregano**

2 **bay leaves**

1 1/2 cups **low-sodium chicken broth**

1 (15 ounces) can crushed **whole tomatoes**

2 teaspoons **Worcestershire sauce**

2 thinly sliced **green onions**, plus extra for garnish

Juice of 1/2 lemon

1 tablespoon **vegetable oil**

1 1/2 pounds **peeled & deveined shrimp**

Cooked **white rice**, for serving

DIRECTIONS:

Melt the butter in a large skillet on medium heat. Sauté the onion, celery, and pepper for five minutes; season with salt and pepper.

Stir in garlic, oregano, paprika, cayenne, and thyme; cook for 1-2 minutes longer until fragrant. Stir in bay leaf and chicken broth; bring to a boil.

Reduce heat and bring to a simmer for 6 to 8 minutes or until the liquid has reduced by one-fourth.

Stir in tomatoes and cook for ten minutes or until the mixture has reduced by half.

Add the Worcestershire sauce and green onions; cook for 10 minutes longer until thickened.

Season the mixture with salt and pepper if the taste needs adjustment; turn off heat and add the lemon juice. Set aside.

Heat the oil in another large pan and cook the shrimp for two minutes on each side or until pinkish. Season shrimp with salt and pepper and pour over the sauce.

Sprinkle on top with green onions. Serve shrimp with cooked rice.

Enjoy!

Nutritional Information: 193 calories; 8.4 g fat (4.2 g saturated fat); 137 mg cholesterol; 9.7 g carbohydrates; 3.2 g dietary fiber; 4.3 g total sugars; 530 mg sodium; 20.4 g protein.

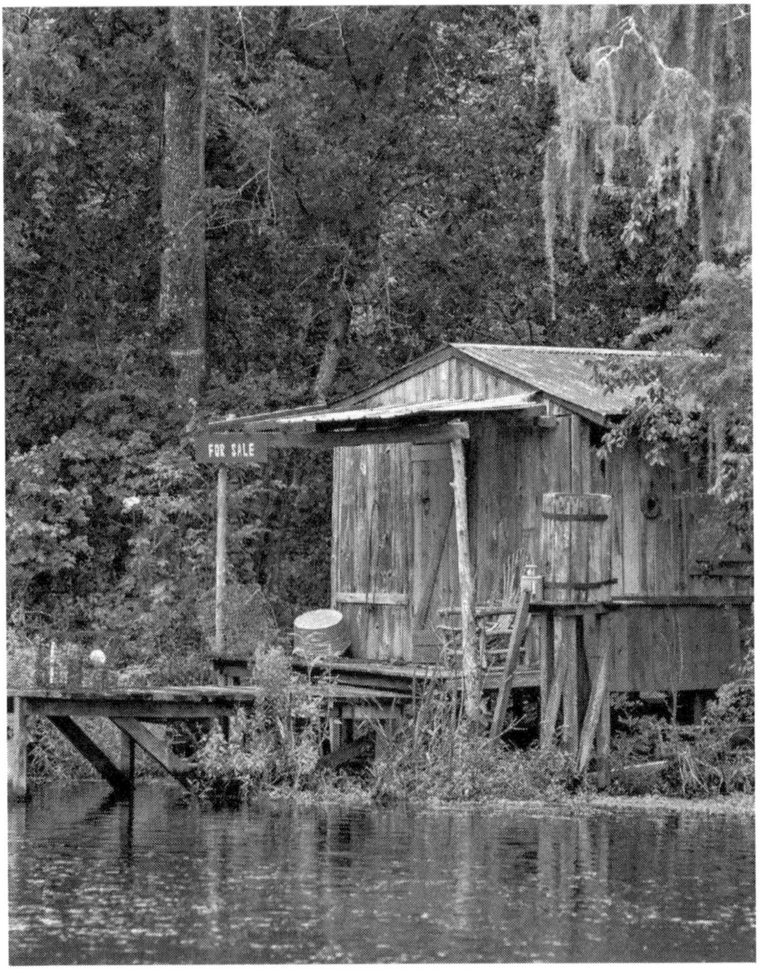
FOR SALE

CHEESY SHRIMP AND GRITS

Enjoy this comforting shrimp soaked in a spicy-tangy creamy sauce. The grits are cooked in chicken broth with cheese, butter and seasonings, and served with chopped fried bacon and tangy shrimp on top.

Servings: 6

Ingredients

2 cups **water**

2 cups **low-sodium chicken broth**

Kosher salt

1 cup **corn grits**

1 cup **shredded cheddar**

4 tablespoons **butter**

Freshly ground **black pepper**

6 slices **bacon**

1 pound **peeled and deveined large shrimp**

1/4 teaspoon **paprika**

1 teaspoon **dried oregano**

4 thinly sliced **green onions**, plus more for garnish

2 minced **cloves garlic**

Juice of 1/2 lemon

Directions

Place the water and chicken broth in a medium saucepan and bring to a boil.

Season the mixture generously with salt and simmer on low, whisking in grits. Stir often and simmer for ten minutes until the grits are soft and the liquid is absorbed.

Stir in cheese and butter; season with salt and pepper.

Cook the bacon in a large pan on medium heat for eight minutes. Drain on a plate lined with paper towel, leaving two tablespoon of bacon fat in pan.

Chop the bacon into small bits. Season the shrimp with paprika and oregano.

Add the shrimp, garlic, and green onions to the skillet; cook and stir for 4 minutes until the shrimp is cooked thoroughly and pink in color. Add lemon juice to shrimp.

Place the grits on a serving platter and top the shrimp and chopped bacon.

Serve!

Nutritional Information: 290 calories; 17.1 g fat (8.3 g saturated fat); 126 mg cholesterol; 8.9 g carbohydrates; 0.9 g dietary fiber; 0.5 g total sugars; 945 mg sodium; 25.5 g protein.

Easy Shrimp & Sausage Gumbo

There's a lot of hype about this Louisiana origin stew. Aside from its thick roux surrounded with celery, onions, and bell peppers, the gumbo is loaded with sausage, Cajun seasoning, spices, shrimp, and green onions that are a match made in heaven.

Servings: 4

Ingredients

4 tablespoons **butter**

1/4 cup **all-purpose flour**

1 chopped medium **green bell pepper**

1 small **yellow onion**

2 chopped **celery ribs**

12 ounces **Andouille sausage**, sliced into 1/2" pieces

2 minced **cloves garlic**

Freshly ground **black pepper**

Kosher salt

1 tablespoon salt less **Cajun seasoning**

1 **bay leaf**

1 (15-ounces) can **fire-roasted diced tomatoes**

4 cups **chicken broth**

1 pound **peeled & deveined shrimp**

3 sliced **green onions**

Cooked white rice, for serving

Directions

Melt the butter in a large, deep pan on medium-low heat.

Add the flour to the pan, stirring often and cook for ten minutes until it turns a dark caramel. Stir in onions, celery, and bell pepper; cook for 5 minutes longer until softened.

Add the sausage and garlic, stir to combine and then stir in Cajun seasoning, pepper, and salt. Add the bay leaf, chicken broth, and diced tomatoes; bring to a boil. Simmer on low for 1 hour, stirring frequently, until the mixture is thickened.

Add the shrimp during the last minute of cooking time until cooked through and pink. Stir in half of green onions.

Serve on top of cooked rice. Sprinkle on top with green onions.

Enjoy!

Nutritional Information: 578 calories; 36.4 g fat (15.8 g saturated fat); 201 mg cholesterol; 20.5 g carbohydrates; 3.4 g dietary fiber; 6.7 g total sugars; 2462 mg sodium; 42.1 g protein.

Best-Ever Shrimp Étouffée

The ingredients in preparing this creamy Shrimp Étouffée are almost the same with gumbo, yet the taste is unique. The roux is a mix of flour, butter, and oil and the interlude of bell pepper, onion and celery, plus garlic, thyme, and onion.

Servings: 4

Ingredients
2 tablespoons **vegetable oil**

2 tablespoons **butter**

1/4 cup **all-purpose flour**

2 chopped **celery ribs**

1 chopped **green bell pepper**

1 chopped medium **yellow onion**

2 thinly sliced **green onions**, plus extra for garnish

3 minced **cloves garlic**

2 teaspoons freshly chopped **thyme**

1 teaspoon **sweet paprika**

1 tablespoon **Cajun seasoning**

Freshly ground **black pepper**

Kosher salt

4 cups **shrimp** or **seafood stock**

1 **bay leaf**

1 1/2 pounds **shelled & deveined shrimp**

White rice, for serving

Directions

Mix together in a large Dutch oven the oil and butter over medium heat.

Whisk the flour in melted and foamy butter until smooth; cook and stir often for 5-6 minutes until the roux is nicely golden.

Stir in onion, celery, and pepper; cook and stir often for 4-5 minutes until softened.

Add the garlic, thyme, and green onions; cook for 1 minute longer until fragrant. Add Cajun seasoning to the mixture, stir to combine; season with paprika, salt, and pepper.

Pour the shrimp or seafood stock one cup at a time, whisking every addition.

Simmer mixture on low and stir in bay leaf. Cover, cook and stir often for 10 to 12 minutes until the veggies are soft and 1/3 of the sauce is absorbed.

Add the shrimp and bring to a simmer; cook and stir often for 4 to 6 minutes until the shrimp is pink and thoroughly cooked.

Discard the bay leaf; season with additional salt and pepper if desired.

Spoon the shrimp and sauce over cooked rice and top with green onions.

Enjoy!

Nutritional Information: 393 calories; 17.8 g fat (5.5 g saturated fat); 274 mg cholesterol; 13.4 g carbohydrates; 2.2 g dietary fiber; 3.2 g total sugars; 757 mg sodium; 42 g protein.

New Orleans Gumbo with Shrimp and Sausage

This New Orleans origin Gumbo is not at all complicated; all you have to do is to prepare the roux before adding the bell peppers, celery, and onions, and then the sausage, spices, tomatoes, broth, and Cajun seasoning. Shrimp and gumbo files follow next.

Servings: 8-10

Ingredients

For the roux:

1/2 cup **high heat oil (canola, corn, or vegetable)**

1/2 cup **all-purpose flour**

For the gumbo:

1 diced medium **onion**

1/2 diced **red bell pepper**

1/2 diced **green bell pepper**

1/2 diced **yellow bell pepper**

1/2 diced **orange bell pepper**

3 diced **stalks celery**

6 minced **cloves garlic**

3 **bay leaves**

8 ounces sliced **Andouille sausage**

1 tablespoon **Cajun seasoning**

1 tablespoon **cayenne**

1 tablespoon **Tabasco sauce**

4 cups **low sodium chicken broth**

1 (14.5 ounce can) roughly diced **stewed tomatoes and juices**

1 1/2 pounds **raw shrimp**

2 teaspoons **gumbo file**

Sliced **scallions**

Cooked **white rice** or **quinoa**

Directions
Make the Roux:

In a heavy bottom pot or large Dutch oven, heat the oil on medium high, and whisk in the flour until smooth and incorporated. Stir often for 15 to 22 minutes using a wooden spoon until the roux is deep, rich brown color, but not burnt.

Add the onions, celery, and bell peppers; stir and cook for 8 to 10 minutes until softened.

Stir in garlic, bay leaves and Andouille sausage. Cook for 1 to 2 minutes more until the garlic is fragrant.

Stir in Tabasco sauce, Cajun seasoning, cayenne, stewed tomatoes, and chicken broth. Bring mixture to a high simmer and then reduce the heat to medium-low; cover and simmer for 15 to 20 minutes longer.

Stir in shrimp and simmer for 10 to 15 minutes more or until the vegetables are softened and the shrimp turns opaque.

Stir in gumbo file and discard the bay leaves.

Serve gumbo with cooked quinoa or white rice. Garnish on top with sliced scallions.

Enjoy!

Nutritional Information: 310 calories; 18.6 g fat (3.4 g saturated fat); 156 mg cholesterol; 12.9 g carbohydrates; 1.6 g dietary fiber; 3.1 g total sugars; 511 mg sodium; 22.3 g protein.

Main Courses

Best-Ever Fried Catfish

These fried catfish fillets deserve to be called as the best ever as far as its taste and flavor is concerned. It has retained its juicy texture even if dredged in a combination of cornmeal and flour mixture. It's crispy outside and oozing with great flavors inside.

Servings: 6

Ingredients
For the Fish:

1 tablespoon **hot sauce**, plus more for serving

2 cup **buttermilk**

1 teaspoon freshly ground **black pepper**

1 teaspoon **kosher salt**

1 1/2 pounds **catfish fillets**

Vegetable oil, for frying

1 **lemon**, sliced into wedges

For dredging:

1/4 cup **all-purpose flour**

1 1/2 cups **yellow cornmeal**

1 teaspoon freshly ground **black pepper**

1 tablespoon **kosher salt**

1/2 teaspoon **garlic powder**

1/2 teaspoon **paprika**

Directions

Place in a Ziploc bag the hot sauce, buttermilk, black pepper, and salt, and add the catfish. Seal the plastic bag, shaking to coat well and chill for 2 to 8 hours.

When ready to cook, whisk in a large shallow bowl the flour, cornmeal, garlic powder, paprika, salt, and pepper.

Working in batches, remove the fish fillet from the buttermilk marinade, shaking off excess.

Dredge the fillet in cornmeal mixture and arrange on a large plate or baking sheet. Repeat the steps until all the catfish fillets are dredged.

Heat the vegetable oil in a Dutch oven or large pot, about halfway, on medium heat or until the oil temperature is at 350 degrees F.

Fry the catfish fillet in batches for 5-6 minutes until golden brown. Drain on paper towels; season with salt.

Serve catfish fillet with hot sauce and lemon wedges alongside.

Enjoy!

Nutritional Information: 341 calories; 12.8 g fat (2.7 g saturated fat); 57 mg cholesterol; 33 g carbohydrates; 2.9 g dietary fiber; 4.5 g total sugars; 1668 mg sodium; 23.6 g protein.

Easy Cajun Jambalaya

This absolutely delicious New Orleans original dish is teeming with the best flavors in town. Keep the shrimp tail intact when cooking this dish as it gives additional seafood flavors to your rice and cooking liquid.

Servings: 4

Ingredients

1 tablespoon **extra-virgin olive oil**

2 chopped **bell peppers**

1 chopped **onion**

Freshly ground **black pepper**

Kosher salt

1 pound **boneless skinless & chicken breasts** cut into 1" pieces

1 teaspoon **dried oregano**

2 minced **cloves garlic**

6 ounces sliced **Andouille sausage**

2 tablespoons **tomato paste**

1 (15 ounces) can crushed **tomatoes**

2 teaspoons **Old Bay seasoning**

1 cup **long grain rice**

2 cups **low-sodium chicken stock**

1 pound **peeled & deveined medium shrimp**

2 thinly sliced **green onions**

Directions

Heat the oil in a large pot on medium heat.

Cook the onion and bell peppers for five minutes in hot oil, until soft; season with salt and pepper.

Add the chicken, cook for five minutes until golden and season with salt, oregano, and pepper. Add the Andouille sausage, tomato paste, and garlic, stirring for 1 minute longer until fragrant.

Stir in chicken broth, Old Bay, rice, and crushed tomatoes. Simmer on medium low, covered, and cook for 20 minutes or until the cooking liquid is almost reduced and the rice is tender. Stir in shrimp and cook for 3-5 minutes until pink.

Sprinkle on top with green onions.

Serve!

Nutritional Information: 625 calories; 17.2 g fat (4.7 g saturated fat); 212 mg cholesterol; 57.2 g carbohydrates; 6.2 g dietary fiber; 11.7 g total sugars; 1527 mg sodium; 60.6 g protein.

Cajun Chicken

This sumptuous New Orleans dish will surely drop your jaw. Each baked chicken is stuffed with sautéed vegetable mixture, cheese, and seasoned with Cajun seasoning. Prep and cooking time is less than an hour.

Servings: 4

Ingredients
2 tablespoons **extra-virgin olive oil**

1 cup diced **red and green bell peppers**

1 cup diced medium **onion**

Freshly ground **black pepper**

Kosher salt

4 **boneless & skinless chicken breasts**

1 cup **shredded cheddar**

2 tablespoons **Cajun seasoning**

Directions

Preheat the oven at 350 degrees F.

Heat the oil in a large oven resistant skillet set on moderate heat.

Add the bell peppers and onions to the skillet; cook for five minutes until soft. Season the mixture with salt and pepper; remove from heat to slightly cool.

Using a sharp knife, make a pocket in the chicken breast and stuff with the sautéed vegetable mixture.

Sprinkle with Cheddar and season with black pepper, Cajun seasoning, and pepper.

Place the chicken to the same skillet and bake for 25 minutes until well done.

Serve!

Nutritional Information: 251 calories; 10.6 g fat (2.2 g saturated fat); 72 mg cholesterol; 5.5 g carbohydrates; 1 g dietary fiber; 2.9 g total sugars; 364 mg sodium; 33.9 g protein.

Cajun BBQ Chicken

This easy and delicious chicken barbecue is just want you want for your dinner. With its simplicity in preparation, the flavorful taste lies in the perfect blending of Cajun seasoning, beer, BBQ sauce, Worcestershire sauce, lime juice, hot sauce, and red pepper flakes.

Servings: 4

Ingredients

1 tablespoon **extra-virgin olive oil**
1 pound **boneless & skinless chicken breast**

1 teaspoon **dried oregano**

2 teaspoons **Cajun seasoning**, divided

Freshly ground **black pepper**

Kosher salt

1 tablespoon **butter**

2 minced **cloves garlic**

1/4 cup **beer**

1/2 cup **barbecue sauce**

Juice of 1 lime

1 tablespoon **Worcestershire sauce**

Dash of **hot sauce**

Pinch of crushed **red pepper flakes**

1/4 cup sliced **green onions**

Cooked rice, for serving

Directions

Heat the oil in a large skillet on medium heat.

Season the chicken breasts all over with oregano, 1 teaspoon Cajun seasoning, salt, and pepper.

Place the chicken in the skillet; cook for six to eight minutes on each side until golden. Remove from heat and set aside.

Melt the butter in the same skillet and cook the garlic for 30 seconds until fragrant.

Stir in barbecue sauce, Worcestershire sauce, beer, red pepper flakes, lime juice, hot sauce and remaining Cajun seasoning. Bring to a boil and simmer on low for five minutes.

Return the chicken to the skillet; simmer for additional 3-5 minutes.

Sprinkle the chicken with chopped green onions. Serve over cooked rice.

Enjoy!

Nutritional Information: 245 calories; 8.1 g fat (2.3 g saturated fat); 73 mg cholesterol; 15.6 g carbohydrates; 1 g dietary fiber; 9.4 g total sugars; 557 mg sodium; 26.8 g protein.

Cajun Parmesan Salmon

These salmon fillets will be added to your favorite dish once your loved ones tasted them. The sauce gives magic touch to the salmon and blended with broth, Cajun seasoning, lemon juice, Parmesan, and honey with lemon slices and parsley.

Servings: 4

Ingredients

1 tablespoon **extra-virgin olive oil**

4 (4 ounces) **fillets (wild) salmon**

2 teaspoons **Cajun seasoning**, divided

Freshly ground **black pepper**

3 minced **cloves garlic**

2 tablespoons **butter**

1 tablespoon **honey**

Juice of 1 lemon

1/3 cup **low-sodium chicken** or **vegetable broth**

2 tablespoons freshly **grated Parmesan**

1 tablespoon freshly chopped **parsley**, plus extra for garnish

Lemon slices for serving

Directions

Heat the oil in a large skillet on medium high.

Season the salmon fillets with pepper and 1 teaspoon Cajun seasoning.

Place the fish in the skillet, skin side upwards. Cook for six minutes, flipping and cook for two minutes longer until deep golden. Drain on paper towel-lined plate.

Place the butter and garlic together in the same skillet.

When melted, add the broth, honey, lemon juice, 1 teaspoon Cajun seasoning, Parmesan, and parsley; bring to a simmer.

Adjust the heat to medium and return the salmon to the skillet. Bring mixture to a simmer for 3-5 minutes or until the salmon is thoroughly cooked and the sauce is almost absorbed.

Place the lemon slices in the skillet before serving.

Enjoy!

Nutritional Information: 167 calories; 12.7 g fat (5.5 g saturated fat); 33 mg cholesterol; 6.8 g carbohydrates; 0.5 g dietary fiber; 4.7 g total sugars; 154 mg sodium; 8.5 g protein.

Cajun Shrimp with Bell Peppers & Corn

This is the quickest way to prepare a Cajun-Creole inspired pasta dish by sautéing the vegetables and add them later to the sautéed shrimp seasoned with Cajun seasoning, salt, and pepper. A sprinkle of lemon juice and parsley to the shrimp should not be missed out before serving.

Servings: 4

Ingredients

2 tablespoons **extra-virgin olive oil**, divided

1/2 (about 1 cup) chopped **onion**

2 chopped **bell peppers**

2 minced **cloves garlic**

2/3 cups (frozen and defrosted or canned) **corn**

1 1/2 pounds **peeled and deveined shrimp**

2 teaspoons **Cajun seasoning**

Freshly ground **black pepper**

Kosher salt

1 tablespoon **lemon juice**

1 tablespoon freshly chopped **parsley**

Directions

Heat one tablespoon olive oil in a large pan on medium heat.

Sauté the bell peppers and onion for five minutes until tender.

Add the garlic and corn; cook for 1 minute longer. Transfer the mixture to a bowl. Set aside.

Heat the remaining one tablespoon oil in the same pan.

Place the shrimp in a single layer; season with Cajun seasoning, salt, and pepper. Cook for one to two minutes on each side until pink.

Add the vegetable mixture together with lemon juice, tossing to coat well. Sprinkle on top with parsley.

Serve!

Nutritional Information: 222 calories; 7.5 g fat (1.1 g saturated fat); 182 mg cholesterol; 12.7 g carbohydrates; 2.2 g dietary fiber; 5.2 g total sugars; 512 mg sodium; 29.3 g protein.

Cajun Shrimp Kebabs

Skewered lemons and shrimp are perfectly seasoned with olive oil and homemade Cajun spice mix consisting of cayenne, garlic powder, onion powder, oregano, paprika, and salt. They make your BBQ party truly memorable.

Servings: 4-6

Ingredients

2 tablespoons **olive oil**

1 pound **shrimp**

1 teaspoon **cayenne**

1 teaspoon **kosher salt**

1 teaspoon **garlic powder**

1 teaspoon **paprika**

1 teaspoon **oregano**

1 teaspoon **onion powder**

2 **lemons**, sliced thinly crosswise

Directions

Heat up the grill to medium high.

Combine in a small bowl the cayenne, salt, paprika, garlic powder, onion powder, and oregano, stirring until combined.

Toss the shrimp in olive oil and spice mix until coated well.

Thread the shrimp and lemon onto wooden skewers or metal skewers. If using wooden skewers, soak them for twenty minutes before using.

Grill the skewered shrimp and lemon for 4 to 5 minutes, turning once during halfway of cooking, or until the shrimp turns opaque and the lemon is charred.

Serve!

Nutritional Information: 141 calories; 6.1 g fat (1.1 g saturated fat); 159 mg cholesterol; 4.1 g carbohydrates; 0.9 g dietary fiber; 0.8 g total sugars; 573 mg sodium; 17.7 g protein.

Cajun Rice Bake

This New Orleans specialty gives you full satisfaction. The sautéed onion, bell peppers, and garlic are blended with chicken breasts, Andouille sausages, tomato sauce, broth, Cajun seasoning, and cheddar. The rice bake is finally baked in oven and served with green onions.

Servings: 4

Ingredients

1 tablespoon **olive oil**

1/2 chopped **red bell pepper**

1/2 chopped **green bell pepper**

1 chopped medium **onion**

2 **Andouille sausages**

2 minced **cloves garlic**

2 large **chicken breasts**

1 teaspoon **Cajun seasoning**

Freshly ground **black pepper**

Kosher salt

1 1/4 cups **long-grain white rice**

2 cups **chicken stock**

1 (15 ounces) can **tomato sauce**

1 cup **Cheddar cheese**

3 sliced **green onions**

Directions

Preheat the oven at 375 degrees F.

Heat the olive oil in a large ovenproof pan on medium heat.

Cook the bell peppers and onion in hot oil until starting to soften.

Cut the sausages into 1-inch pieces and add to the pan; cook until browned.

Add the garlic and sauté for 30 seconds until fragrant.

Cut the chicken breasts into 1-inch pieces and add to the pan along with Cajun seasoning. Season the mixture with salt and pepper; cook and stir often until the chicken is thoroughly cooked.

Add the rice and pour over the chicken broth and tomato sauce and then stir in the cheddar. Simmer mixture and transfer to the oven.

Bake for 35 to 45 minutes until the rice is thoroughly cooked. Slightly cool the rice bake in pan for five to ten minutes.

Sprinkle on top with sliced green onions.

Enjoy!

Nutritional Information: 518 calories; 17.4 g fat (7.7 g saturated fat); 83 mg cholesterol; 59.8 g carbohydrates; 3.7 g dietary fiber; 8 g total sugars; 1320 mg sodium; 29.2 g protein.

NEW ORLEANS BBQ SHRIMP

New Orleans cuisine brings total satisfaction in every party. This BBQ shrimp makes your tongue drool with its fusion of buttery, tangy and spicy flavors from the mixture of hot sauce, Worcestershire sauce, beer, creole seasoning, and butter.

Servings: 2

Ingredients

2 tablespoons **butter**

3 chopped **cloves garlic**

2 teaspoons **creole seasoning**

1/4 cup **Worcestershire sauce**

1/4 cup **hot sauce** or more

2 tablespoons **lemon juice of 1/2 lemon**

1/3 cup **beer**, **wine** or **broth**

1/2 teaspoon ground **black pepper**

1 pound **peeled and deveined shrimp**

2 tablespoons **chilled butter**, cut into 1/2 inch pieces

Salt to taste

Directions

In a pan, melt the butter on medium-high heat and sauté the garlic for 30 seconds until fragrant.

Stir in hot sauce, beer, Worcestershire sauce, lemon juice, pepper, and creole seasoning. Bring mixture to a simmer and cook for 5 to 7 minutes until half of the sauce is reduced.

Place the shrimp in the mixture and cook for 2 to 3 minutes on each side until cooked through. Simmer on medium-low and stir in cold butter until melted.

Sprinkle with salt if desired. Serve with French bread.

Enjoy!

Nutritional Information: 487 calories; 23 g fat (14 g saturated fat); 489 mg cholesterol; 12 g carbohydrates; 0.5 g dietary fiber; 4 g total sugars; 1329 mg sodium; 55 g protein.

Red Beans and Rice with Ground Beef

This authentic Louisiana dish is replete with all the flavors and nutrients you need to make your meal a pleasure. Each bowl of cooked rice is topped with aromatic red beans and beef mixture flavored with Cajun seasoning and sautéed vegetables.

Servings: 8

Ingredients

3 **celery ribs**

2 **green peppers**

2 tablespoons minced **garlic**

1 medium **onion**

1/4 cup **bacon fat**

2 teaspoons **Cajun seasoning**

1 pound **ground beef**

4 cans **kidney beans**

1 (14 ounces) package **beef sausage**

2 cup **chicken** or **beef broth**

8 cups **hot cooked rice**

Directions

Heat the oil in a 4 quart heavy bottomed pot on medium heat.

Add the onion, garlic, bell pepper, and celery.

Cook the vegetables in bacon fat until softened. Stir in ground beef; cook until browned.

Add the beans and broth to the mixture. Stir in Cajun seasoning and bring to a boil.

Simmer on low heat and stir in sausage; simmer for half an hour. Top the cooked rice with beans.

Serve!

Nutritional Information: 1132 calories; 29.3 g fat (11.9 g saturated fat); 101 mg cholesterol; 167.6 g carbohydrates; 8.5 g dietary fiber; 3.6 g total sugars; 932 mg sodium; 44 g protein.

Slow-Cooker Jambalaya

This insanely delicious jambalaya is cooked in a slow cooker for 4 hours. The chicken, vegetables and sausage are sautéed first before cooking in the slow cooker and right there the tomatoes, broth, Cajun seasoning, and shrimp are added.

Serving: 4

Ingredients

Extra-virgin olive oil

1 pound **boneless skinless chicken breast**, cut into 1" cubes

6 ounces **Andouille sausage**, cut into 1/4" slices

1 chopped **onion**

2 minced **garlic cloves**

2 chopped **celery stalks**

1 tablespoon chopped **fresh thyme**

1 seeded and chopped **jalapeno chili**1 seeded and chopped **green bell pepper**Freshly ground **black pepper**

28 ounces (can) diced **tomatoes**

3 cups **low sodium chicken broth**

2 teaspoons **Cajun seasoning**

12 **peeled and deveined large shrimp**

2 cups **cooked long-grain rice**

Chopped scallions for garnish

Directions

Heat one tablespoon of olive oil in a large pan on medium-high heat.

Cook the chicken in hot oil for 4 to 5 minutes; season with ½ teaspoon salt. Stir often and transfer to a six-quart slow cooker. Set aside.

In the same skillet, lightly brown the sausage for two minutes and transfer to the slow cooker.

Add the onion, garlic, celery, jalapeño, thyme, and green pepper to the skillet. Season the vegetables with ½ teaspoon pepper and 1 teaspoon salt, stirring often for five minutes.

Pour the vegetables to the slow cooker and add the chicken broth, Cajun seasoning, and tomatoes. Cover the cooker and cook for 4 hours on low.

While slow cooking the mixture, cook the shrimp in the same skillet for three minutes on each side on medium-high heat. Season the shrimp with salt and set aside.

Meanwhile, cook the rice according to package directions and add to the slow cooker after 4 hours. Simmer the mixture for 15 minutes.

During the last five minutes of cooking, add the shrimp to slow cooker to warm through.

Garnish jambalaya with chopped scallions.

Enjoy!

Nutritional Information: 905 calories; 26 g fat (7.1 g saturated fat); 300 mg cholesterol; 90.8 g carbohydrates; 5.2 g dietary fiber; 8.7 g total sugars; 875 mg sodium; 74.2 g protein.

Breads & Breakfast Dishes
Shrimp Po'Boy Sliders

These mini sandwiches can feed a dozen people. One slider can give you full satisfaction with its tons of flavors rolled into one. The spicy, tangy and creamy remoulade is spread on the bun, topped with fried shrimp, lettuce, and cherry tomatoes.

Servings: 12

Ingredients

2 large **eggs**

1/2 cup **whole milk**

1/2 cup finely ground **cornmeal**

1/2 cup **all-purpose flour**

1 teaspoon **dried thyme**

1 tablespoon **Cajun seasoning**

Freshly ground **black pepper**

Kosher salt

1 pound **peeled & deveined shrimp**, tails removed

Vegetable oil, for frying

12 **slider buns**

For serving:

Sliced **cherry tomatoes**

Shredded **iceberg lettuce**

For the remoulade:

1 tablespoon **whole-grain mustard**

1 cup **mayonnaise**

1 tablespoon **Louisiana hot sauce**

1 tablespoon **lemon juice**

2 thinly sliced **green onions**

1 tablespoon chopped **parsley**

Directions

Whisk in a large bowl the eggs and milk. Set aside.

Whisk in another large bowl the cornmeal, flour, dried thyme, and Cajun seasoning; season with salt and black pepper.

Dredge the shrimp in egg-milk mixture, tossing in the flour mixture to coat.

Heat about two-inch of oil in a large skillet over medium heat.

When the oil is shimmering, fry the shrimp for two minutes on each side until golden and drain on a plate lined with paper towel.

Prepare the remoulade by whisking in a bowl the mayonnaise, green onions, mustard, parsley, hot sauce, and lemon juice.

Assemble the sliders by spreading the remoulade on the bottom bun.

Top with fried shrimp, and then lettuce, and tomatoes.

Finally, cover with slider bun tops.

Serve!

Nutritional Information: 241 calories; 10.2 g fat (1.7 g saturated fat); 78 mg cholesterol; 27.1 g carbohydrates; 1.8 g dietary fiber; 4.3 g total sugars; 448 mg sodium; 10.8 g protein.

Easy Beignets

If you drop by New Orleans, don't miss out these sugary deep fried fritters. They are not only pleasing to your sweet tooth; they can ease your hunger. This no bake pastry is so easy to prepare and they require less cooking time.

Servings: 15

Ingredients

1 teaspoon **baking powder**

1 1/4 cups **all-purpose flour**

1/8 teaspoon **kosher salt**

1/2 cup **granulated sugar**

2 large **eggs**, separated

1/4 cup **water**

1 teaspoon **pure vanilla extract**

1 tablespoon **melted butter**

Vegetable oil for frying

Powdered sugar for dusting

Directions

Whisk in a large bowl the flour, salt, and baking powder.

Combine in a separate large bowl the egg yolks, ¼ cup water, sugar, vanilla, and melted butter, stirring to combine well.

Add the mixture to the flour mixture until just combined. Set aside.

Using a hand mixer beat in a large bowl the egg whites on medium speed to form into soft peaks and add to the batter.

Heat the oil in a large pot at 375 degrees F.

Using a spoon, drop the batter in batches into the hot oil. Fry for five minutes until golden.

Drain beignets on a plate lined with paper towels.

Sprinkle the beignets with powdered sugar.

Serve!

Nutritional Information: 98 calories; 3.3 g fat (1.1 g saturated fat); 27 mg cholesterol; 15.4 g carbohydrates; 0.3 g dietary fiber; 7.3 g total sugars; 35 mg sodium; 1.9 g protein.

Sauces & Marinades

Louisiana Shrimp Dip

This garlicky and creamy dip is no ordinary dip. Each moment you lick the dip, you can taste the bits of sautéed shrimp cooked in Cajun seasoning, lemon juice, and Worcestershire sauce. Tighten it up with more cream cheese if you desire.

Servings: 8

Ingredients

1 tablespoon **butter**

1 finely chopped **red bell pepper**

1/4 finely chopped **onion**

2 minced **garlic cloves**

1 pound **shrimp**, chopped into 1/2" pieces

1 teaspoon **Worcestershire sauce**

2 tablespoons **lemon juice**

1 teaspoon **Cajun seasoning**

Kosher salt

1/4 cup **sour cream**

6 ounces softened **cream cheese**

1/4 cup **freshly shredded Parmesan**

3/4 cup **shredded mozzarella**, divided

1/4 cup sliced **green onions**, plus more for garnish

Directions

Preheat the oven at 350 degrees F.

Melt the butter in a medium pan on moderate heat.

Cook the bell pepper and onion for five minutes until soft. Push the pepper and onion to the side of the pan.

Add the garlic cloves and shrimp, stirring often and cook for 2 minutes until the garlic is aromatic and the shrimp turns pink.

Stir in Cajun seasoning, Worcestershire sauce, lemon juice, and salt; stir and bring to a simmer.

Remove from heat and quickly stir in sour cream, cream cheese, Parmesan, ½ cup mozzarella, and green onions. Sprinkle on top with the remaining ¼ cup mozzarella cheese.

Bake the dip for 15-20 minutes or until slightly golden and bubbly.

For a dark golden top, you may also broil the dip on high for two minutes. Sprinkle on top with sliced green onions.

Serve!

Nutritional Information: 210 calories; 13.4 g fat (8.1 g saturated fat); 156 mg cholesterol; 4.2 g carbohydrates; 0.4 g dietary fiber; 1.2 g total sugars; 331 mg sodium; 18.1 g protein.

Appetizers & Salads
Cajun Chicken Sausage Alfredo

Twist your pasta into a Cajun and Creole delight by combining the cooked penne with chicken and sausage cooked in a perfect blend of Classic Alfredo Sauce and Cajun seasoning sauce. It is so easy to whip up in 35 minutes.

Servings: 4-6

Ingredients

1 pound **penne**

2 tablespoons **extra-virgin olive oil**

1 thinly sliced **red bell pepper**

2 **chicken breasts** cut into 1" pieces

2 **Andouille sausage**, sliced into 1/2" pieces

Freshly ground **black pepper**

Kosher salt

1 tablespoon **Cajun seasoning**

1 (16 ounces) jar **RAGÚ Classic Alfredo Sauce**

2 thinly sliced **green onions**

Directions

Cook the penne pasta al dente, according to its package directions; drain and set aside.

Heat the olive oil in a large pan over medium heat. Cook the red pepper in hot oil for five minutes until slightly softened.

Add the chicken breasts and cook for 6-8 minutes until thoroughly cooked and golden.

Add the sausage, cook for two minutes longer until warmed thoroughly. Season the mixture with Cajun seasoning, pepper, and salt.

Stir in RAGÚ Classic Alfredo Sauce and bring to a simmer.

Add the cooked penne to the mixture, stirring until combined.

Remove from heat and top with sliced green onions.

Serve!

Nutritional Information: 373 calories; 12.1 g fat (2.8 g saturated fat); 101 mg cholesterol; 44.6 g carbohydrates; 0.4 g dietary fiber; 1.1 g total sugars; 302 mg sodium; 19.4 g protein.

CREOLE POTATO SALAD

This potato salad is an excellent side dish for any occasion with its unique blend of Zatarain's seasoning and vinegar after boiling with Zatarain's crab boil. A mixture of mayonnaise, mustard, sugar and sour cream blends well with eggs, celery, parsley and green onion.

Servings: 10

Ingredients

3 pounds halved or quartered **red potatoes**

1 tablespoon **Zatarain's liquid shrimp and crab boil**, optional

Pinch of **salt**

3/4 teaspoon **Zatarain's Creole seasoning**

1 tablespoon **apple cider vinegar**

1/3 cup **sour cream**

1/3 cup **mayonnaise**

1 teaspoon **sugar**

1/3 cup **Zatarain's Creole mustard**

3 chopped **hard-boiled eggs**

1 finely chopped stalk **celery**

1 tablespoon chopped fresh **parsley**

3 sliced **green onions**

Directions

Fill a large pot with the halved or quartered potatoes. Cover with water, at least an inch above the potatoes.

Pour the Zatarain's crab boil into the pot and sprinkle with a few pinches of salt; bring to a boil. Simmer the potatoes for 15-20 minutes on low heat or until the potatoes are fork tender.

Drain and transfer the potatoes to a large bowl. Toss in Zatarain's seasoning and vinegar. Set aside.

Meanwhile, combine in a small bowl the sour cream, sugar, mustard, and mayonnaise.

Add the dressing to the potatoes, stirring until incorporated; sprinkle with salt and pepper to taste.

Add the eggs, celery, parsley and green onion, stir to combine.

Sprinkle on top with Zatarain's seasoning. Chill.

Serve!

Nutritional Information: 181 calories; 6.5 g fat (1.8 g saturated fat); 55 mg cholesterol; 535.8 g carbohydrates; 2.5 g dietary fiber; 2.6 g total sugars; 367 mg sodium; 4.6 g protein.

CAJUN SPICE

For first timers in Cajun and Creole cooking, this is the basic of preparing Cajun spice mix. The ingredients can be sourced from your pantry. If you love something hotter, just add crushed red pepper.

Servings: 12

Ingredients

2 1/2 teaspoons **paprika**

2 teaspoons **garlic powder**

1 teaspoon **onion powder**

1 teaspoon **ground black pepper**

2 teaspoons **salt**

1 1/4 teaspoons **dried oregano**

1 1/4 teaspoons **dried thyme**

1 teaspoon **cayenne pepper**

1/2 teaspoon **red pepper flakes**

DIRECTIONS:

Combine all ingredients and stir until completely blended.

Store homemade Cajun Spice mixture in an airtight container, and ready for use.

Nutritional Information: 6 calories; 0.1 g fat; 1.2 g carbohydrates; 0.2 g protein; 0 mg cholesterol; 388 mg sodium.

THIBODEAUX GUMBO

This is a classic gumbo that will really perk up your day. It's perfect for hanging out with your buddies by having a cold beer, with steamed rice and corn bread.

Servings: 10

Ingredients

1 tablespoon **olive oil**

1 cup **olive oil**

1 cup chopped skinless and boneless **chicken breast halves**

1/2 pound thinly sliced **pork sausage links**

2 tablespoons minced **garlic**

1 cup **all-purpose flour**

1 can of (12 ounces) **beer**

3 quarts **chicken broth**

4 diced **roma (plum) tomatoes**

1 sliced **sweet onion**

6 stalks diced **celery**

1 bunch chopped fresh **parsley**

1 pound peeled and deveined **shrimp**

1/4 cup **Cajun seasoning**

1 can of (10 ounces) diced **tomatoes with green chili peppers** (with liquid)

2 tablespoons chopped fresh **red chili peppers**

Directions

In a medium skillet, heat oil on medium high heat.

Stir in chicken and cook until pink color and the liquid runs clear.

Add sausage, stir and cook until lightly browned. Remove excess oil in sausage and chicken in paper towel.

In a large saucepan, blend 1 cup olive oil and flour to form a roux. Stir frequently until mixture is bubbly and browned.

Stir in garlic and cook for 1 minute.

Pour beer and chicken broth gradually into the prepared roux mixture, and bring to a boil.

Stir in celery, sweet onion, and tomatoes with green chili peppers, parsley, red chili peppers, Cajun seasoning and parsley. Cover and cook broth mixture over low fire for 40 minutes, stirring frequently.

Add chicken, shrimp and sausage into the mixture, cover and cook for additional 20 minutes, stirring regularly.

Enjoy!

Nutritional Information: 437 calories, 21.7 g protein, 18.5 g carbohydrate, 29.3 g fat ; 105 mg cholesterol, 2052 mg sodium.

Cajun Pasta

This is a simple method of preparing pasta with a twist for a busy person like you. You can prepare it beforehand and presto, you can serve it to your surprise guests.

Servings: 8

Ingredients

2 tablespoons **olive oil**
1 teaspoon minced **garlic**
1 pound **vermicelli pasta**
13 pieces chopped **roma tomatoes**
1 tablespoon **Cajun seasoning**
1/2 cup shredded **mozzarella cheese**
1/2 cup grated **Parmesan cheese**
1 tablespoon chopped **fresh parsley**
1 tablespoon **salt**

Directions

Fill large pot with salted water and bring to a boil.

Add pasta and cook according to package direction, al dente. Drain pasta and set aside.

In a large skillet, sauté garlic in oil until lightly brown.

Add roma tomatoes together with juice and drizzle with salt. Stir mixture until the tomatoes are soft. Mash tomatoes while cooking using a fork.

Add parsley and stir until mixture is blended. Simmer for 5 minutes on low fire, set aside.

Toss pasta with the tomato mixture, Cajun seasoning, and Parmesan and mozzarella cheese. Enjoy!

Nutritional Information: 294 calories; 12.2 g protein; 46.2 g carbohydrate; 7.5 g fat 428; 9 mg cholesterol; 1178 mg sodium.

Cajun Turkey

For non-pork eaters, this Cajun dish will provide you with a satisfying dinner or serve this for your Thanksgiving dinner. It is best served with a savory rice dish and grilled vegetable.

Servings: 6

Ingredients

3-4 pounds boneless and skinless **turkey breast**
2 teaspoons **oil**
2 tablespoons **melted butter**
Cajun Seasoning:
1 teaspoon cracked **black pepper**
2 teaspoons **onion powder**
2 teaspoons **paprika**
1 1/2 teaspoons **salt**
1 teaspoon **dried thyme**
1/2 teaspoon **garlic powder**
1/2 teaspoon **ground cumin**
1/2 teaspoon **cayenne pepper**

Directions

Combine oil, butter and Cajon seasoning ingredients and stir until well blended.

Rub mixture over meat to coat. Place meat in a baking dish lined with parchment.

Roast seasoned turkey breast in 375 degrees F oven to an internal oven temperature at 170 degrees F.

Let roasted turkey breast rest for 10 minutes before slicing.

Serve!

Nutritional Information: 497 calories; 81 g protein; 12 g carbohydrate; 13 g fat; 200 mg cholesterol; 165 mg sodium.

LOUISIANA BOUDIN

Sausage comes in a variety of forms, and Louisianans are proud to have this unique version of their sausage, which is stuffed with rice and pork or you can add catfish or prawns for your own version.

Servings: 18

Ingredients

1 pound cubed **pork liver**

2 1/2 pounds cubed boneless **pork shoulder**

2 cups **white rice**, uncooked

4 cups **water**

Additional 4 cups of **water**

1 cup chopped **onion**

1 1/4 cups chopped **green onions**

2 1/2 teaspoons **cayenne pepper**

1 1/2 teaspoons ground **black pepper**

1/2 teaspoon **red pepper flakes**

2 tablespoons minced **cilantro**

1 teaspoon minced **garlic**

1/2 cup minced **celery**

1 chopped red **bell pepper**

1 cup chopped fresh **parsley**

4 teaspoons **salt**

4 feet length **hog casings** with 1 1/2 inch diameter

Directions

Clean the hog casing by rinsing it with warm water inside and out. Let sausage casings stay in warm water until ready to use.

In a large saucepan, pour 4 cups of water and place liver and pork shoulder. Cover and bring to a boil. Simmer meat on medium low fire for 1 ½ hours until pork cubes are soft.

In a separate saucepan, boil rice with 4 cups of water, cover and simmer on medium low heat until liquid is absorbed and rice is palatable for 20 to 25 minutes. Set aside.

Remove pork cubes and liver from saucepan using a slotted spoon. Let it cool and set aside.

Stir in onion, green onion, bell pepper, celery, cilantro, garlic and parsley in pork cubes and liver broth.

Season broth with cayenne pepper, black pepper, and salt, and red pepper flakes, cook for a minute until the onion is soft.

Grind the cooked meat with a meat grinder using the coarse plate.

Add the ground meat in the broth, cover and cook. Stir frequently until the broth is reduced for about 10 minutes.

Stir in the boiled rice. Set aside and cool.

Stuff sausage mixture into the clean hog casings using a stuffer; prick each sausage with a needle every 4-5 inches.

In a large pot, boil enough salted water on high heat. Lower the fire and add the sausage, cook in simmering water until inside of sausage are warm, firm and plumped for 5 minutes.

Serve!

Nutritional Information: 188 calories; 11.2 g protein; 20 g carbohydrate; 6.6 g fat; 64 mg cholesterol, 551 mg sodium.

CAJUN PRAWNS

This dish is so simple to make and the ingredients are right from your pantry. Dance to the beat of reggae and shake the ingredients, then fry the prawns. There you have your dinner!

Servings: 4

Ingredients

1 tablespoon **vegetable oil**
1 1/2 pounds peeled and deveined **prawns**
1/4 teaspoon **garlic powder**
1/4 teaspoon **ground black pepper**
1 teaspoon **paprika**
3/4 teaspoon **dried thyme**
1/4 teaspoon **cayenne pepper**
3/4 teaspoon **dried oregano**
1/4 teaspoon **salt**

Directions

In a resealable plastic bag, combine thyme, paprika, garlic powder, oregano, pepper, cayenne pepper and salt.

Shake to blend all ingredients. Place prawns inside the bag and shake to evenly coat.

In a large skillet, heat oil on medium high heat.

Stir in prawns until they turn dark pink, and center is no longer transparent for about 4 minutes.

Serve!

Nutritional Information: 945 calories; 155.7 g protein; 13.8 g carbohydrate; 25.7 g fat; 1433 mg cholesterol; 2243 mg sodium.

Savour Press's Classical Creole Chicken

This spicy chicken thighs taste so good and time saving. You can do other tasks while waiting for the chicken and Spanish rice to cook. If you want it hot, just add red pepper flakes.

Servings: 4

Ingredients

4 skinless **chicken thighs**
2 tablespoons **butter**
1 pinch **Creole seasoning**
1 can of (15 ounces) diced **tomatoes with green chili peppers**
1 can of (8 ounce) **tomato sauce**
1 cup **water**
1 package (6.8 ounce) **Spanish-style rice mix**

Directions

Season the chicken thighs with a pinch of Creole seasoning.

In a skillet on medium heat, melt butter and cook chicken until golden brown, turning each side for 3 to 4 minutes. Remove chicken from skillet, set aside.

In the same skillet, stir in tomatoes with green chili peppers, tomato sauce, water and Spanish-style rice mix.

Add the cooked chicken thighs to the rice mixture; cover and bring to a boil.

Simmer chicken over low heat until pink color disappears and rice is cooked for 40 minutes. Serve creole on a platter with chicken over rice.

Enjoy!

Nutritional Information: 400 calories, 27.3 g protein, 41.9 g carbohydrate, 14.2 g fat ; 93 mg cholesterol, 1751 mg sodium.

Baton Rouge Gravy

Serve this recipe with sausage and biscuits to make your meal more enjoyable.

Servings: 6

Ingredients

1/2 cup **vegetable oil**
1 chopped **onion**
3/4 cup **all-purpose flour**
1 teaspoon **ground black pepper**
4 cups **milk**
1 chopped **onion**
1 teaspoon **salt**

Directions

In a large skillet, heat oil on medium heat.

Whisk in flour, pepper, salt and chopped onion until mixture becomes smooth.

Cook mixture and stir frequently until lightly brown for 10 minutes.

Stir milk gradually to prevent lump formation until mixture is thickened.

Add a few drops of milk in case the gravy is too thick.

Serve with Cajun!

Nutritional Information: 300 calories, 7 g protein, 19.8 g carbohydrate, 21.5 g fat 77.1 mg cholesterol, 1263.9 mg sodium.

CREOLE CAKE

Tired of commercial cakes from fast food outlets? Why not create your own creole cake? This cake is so moist and quick to prepare.

Servings: 12

Ingredients

1/2 cup **vegetable oil**

2 **eggs**

2 cup **cocoa**

2 cups **sugar**

1 teaspoon **baking soda**

2 cups **flour**

1/2 cup **buttermilk**

1 tablespoon **vanilla**

1 cup **boiling water**

Frosting

1 1/2cups packed **brown sugar**

4 cups melted **margarine**

2/3 cups **evaporated milk**

3/4 cups chopped **pecans**

1 cup **angel flake coconut**

1 teaspoon **vanilla**

Directions

Preheat oven at 325 degrees Fahrenheit.

In a large mixing bowl, combine cocoa, sugar, baking soda and flour until completely blended.

Whisk eggs, milk, vanilla and oil on low speed in your mixer.

Add boiling water and continue whisking the egg mixture until it becomes thin.

Pour mixture into a greased and floured 9x 13 inch baking pan.

Bake mixture for 30 to 35 minutes until toothpick comes out clean.

Mix frosting ingredients and spread evenly on top of cake.

Place cake under broiler for 1 to 2 minutes until it begins to brown.

Cool cake before slicing.

Nutritional Information: 12481 calories; 94.6 g protein; 943.7 g carbohydrate; 909.7 g fat; 381mg cholesterol; 10321 mg sodium.

CREOLE MEATLOAF

Canned meatloaf is high in preservatives and additives, but this homemade meatloaf is different. It is all natural, and with a balance of spice and sweet, you got your yummy meatloaf right from your kitchen.

Servings: 4

Ingredients

1/4 cup crushed and drained **pineapple**
1/3 cup **ketchup**
1 pound **ground beef**
1 beaten **egg**
1/4 cup **brown sugar**
1/4 cup **bacon bit**
1 dash **Worcestershire sauce**
3/4 teaspoon **salt**
1/4 cup dry **bread crumbs**
1/2 clove minced **garlic**
1/4 minced **onion**
1/4 teaspoon **ground black pepper**
2 dashes **Worcestershire sauce**
1/4 cup crushed **saltine crackers**

Directions

Preheat oven at 350 ° Fahrenheit. In a small bowl, combine brown sugar, ketchup, pineapple, bacon bits and dash of Worcestershire sauce, set aside.

In a large mixing bowl, combine bread crumbs, ground beef, egg, onion, saltines, salt, pepper and 2 dashes of Worcestershire sauce, and garlic, blend well.

Place meat into a loaf pan, about 9x5 inch.

Bake meatloaf for 30 minutes. Remove meatloaf from oven.

Pour reserved pineapple juice on top of meatloaf.

Place meatloaf in oven, bake until meat is thoroughly cooked for 20 minutes more.

Serve!

Nutritional Information: 401 calories; 20.1 g fat; 30.7 g carbohydrates; 24.5 g protein; 120 mg cholesterol; 1047 mg sodium.

Crawfish and Shrimp

Gumbo recipes evolved into different versions, but here is a simple yet super tasty dish that will answer all your cravings.

Servings: 8

Ingredients

- ⅓ cups **vegetable oil**
- 1 cup minced **white onion**
- 1 medium seeded and chopped **green bell pepper**
- 1 medium seeded and chopped **red bell pepper**
- 1 cup chopped **celery**
- 5 minced cloves **garlic**
- ½ cup **all-purpose flour**
- 8 cups **water**
- 2 tablespoons **Cajun seasoning**
- 1 can of (28-ounce) diced **fire-roasted tomatoes with liquid**
- 1 pound large peeled and deveined **Louisiana shrimp with tails**
- 2 cups sliced fresh **okra**
- 2 packages (16-ounce) undrained cooked **Louisiana crawfish tails**

For serving:

Hot cooked rice

For garnish:

Chopped parsley and sliced green onion

Directions

Heat vegetable oil on medium heat for about 5 minutes in a Dutch oven.

Whisk flour until fully combined in oven.

Reduce heat to medium low and continue cooking, stirring occasionally, until roux forms for 30 to 40 minutes.

Stir in onion, celery and bell peppers until onion is transparent for about 15 minutes.

Stir in garlic for 30 seconds. Pour 8 cups of water, Cajun seasoning and tomato.

Bring mixture to a boil, simmer for an hour. Stir in shrimp, crawfish, and okra, and bring to a boil.

Reduce heat and simmer for 15 minutes.

Serve with hot cooked rice and top with green onion and parsley.

Enjoy!

Nutritional Information: 2148 calories; 204 g protein; 129.1 g carbohydrate; 89.6 g fat ; 1577 mg cholesterol;1968 mg sodium.

Cajun Burger

Your kids love to eat burgers, but their price is so costly. Why not prepare your own burger with this recipe. Just adjust the measurement and filling according to your kid's taste.

Servings: 4

Ingredients

Cajun seasoning blend:

1 tablespoon **paprika**

1 teaspoon **cayenne pepper**

1 tablespoon **garlic powder**

3 tablespoons **dried oregano**

3 tablespoons **ground cumin**

2 teaspoons **salt**

Burgers:

1 pound **ground beef**

1 minced **garlic clove**

1/4 cup onion, finely **chopped**

1/2 to 1 teaspoon **hot pepper sauce**

1/2 teaspoon **dried thyme**

1/4 teaspoon **dried basil**

1 teaspoon **Cajun seasoning blend**

1 teaspoon **salt**

4 **hamburger buns**

Optional:

Sautéed onions

Directions

In a resealable plastic bag or a bowl, combine Cajun seasoning blend ingredients, stir until fully blended.

In a large mixing bowl, mix altogether the burger ingredients. Form them into 4 patties.

Grill on medium high heat for about 4 to 5 minutes each side until patties reach their doneness.

Fill buns with patties and top with sautéed onions.

Keep the remaining Cajun seasoning blend in a sealed container for future use.

Serve!

Nutritional Information: 394 calories; 28 g protein; 29 g carbohydrate; 18 g fat; 75 mg cholesterol; 2246 mg sodium.

Cajun Breakfast

Mornings could be difficult for busy homemakers. This recipe will solve your breakfast. It can be prepared in advanced and keep refrigerated. By the next morning your breakfast is ready.

Servings: 6 to 8

Ingredients

3 tablespoons **olive oil**
1 medium diced **onion**
6 **eggs**
Butter to grease pan
4 cups loosely packed **cornbread** (cut into 1 inch cubes)
1 diced **green pepper**
½ pound of medium diced **Andouille sausage**
1 teaspoon minced **garlic**
¼ teaspoon **cayenne pepper**
¼ teaspoon **black pepper**
1½ cup **whole milk**
1 cup shredded **cheese**
½ teaspoon **salt**

Directions

Preheat oven at 350 ° Fahrenheit.

Place cornbread in a greased 2 ½ quart baking dish, set aside. In a large skillet, heat olive oil on medium heat.

Stir in onion, Andouille sausage, and pepper, cook until green peppers are tender and onion is transparent, stirring frequently.

Stir in garlic, peppers and salt until fully combined. Set aside.

In a mixing bowl, combine milk, eggs and cheese, set aside.

Spread sausage and pepper mixture on top of cornbread, and pour milk mixture on top.

Bake for about an hour without a cover until the edges are bubbly and top turns lightly brown.

Test Cajun with a toothpick and when it comes out clean; your breakfast is now cooked.

Serve!

Nutritional Information: 3026 calories; 154.8 g protein; 119.4 g carbohydrate; 216.3 g fat; 1390 mg cholesterol; 5945 mg sodium.

Cajun Bisque

Brunch and snacks would be enjoyable with this comfort food that you can serve when the season is cold. This soup will keep your body warm, and fill your hungry stomach.

Servings: 8

Ingredients

1 tablespoon **vegetable oil**
3 tablespoons **butter**
1/4 cup chopped **green onions**
1 large chopped **onion**
1 tablespoon minced **garlic**
3 tablespoons **all-purpose flour**
1 large minced **celery stalk**
Cajun seasoning
1 cup **chicken broth**
1 1/2 cups frozen **corn kernels**
1 **bay leaf**
2 cups **milk**
2 cups **heavy cream**
1 teaspoon **liquid shrimp and crab boil seasoning**
1 pound fresh **lump crabmeat**
1/2 teaspoon **Worcestershire sauce**
Pinch of **salt**
Dash of **pepper**
Chopped **green onions**

Directions

In a saucepan, melt butter on medium heat.

Whisk flour gradually into saucepan, cook for 5 to 7 minutes, and whisk frequently to form golden roux, set aside.

In a Dutch oven, heat oil on medium heat.

Stir in onion, garlic and celery and cook for 1 minute.

Pour Cajun seasoning. Stir in corn, broth and bay leaf, simmer.

Add cream, milk and liquid crab boil. Lower heat when mixture simmers. Continue cooking for 7 minutes.

Slowly add roux and blend mixture thoroughly. Whisk mixture until thickens.

Add green onions, Worcestershire sauce and crabmeat, stirring frequently, for 6 to 8 minutes.

Season the bisque with pepper and salt.

Enjoy!

Nutritional Information: 387 calories; 14.8 g protein; 16.3 g carbohydrate; 30.1 g fat; 131 mg cholesterol; 278 mg sodium.

Jambalaya

Jambalaya is a popular dish that has penetrated to other cultures. This version recipe will make you dance with the infusion of Andouille sausage and chicken that can satiate your hunger.

Servings: 6

Ingredients

1 tablespoon **Cajun seasoning**

1 diced **onion**

3 cloves minced **garlic**

1 small diced **green bell pepper**

2 tablespoons **peanut oil**, divided

1 pound sliced boneless skinless **chicken breasts**

10 ounces sliced **Andouille sausage**

1 can (16 ounce) crushed **Italian tomatoes**

1/2 teaspoon ground **black pepper**

1/2 teaspoon **hot pepper sauce**

2 teaspoons **Worcestershire sauce**

1 teaspoon **file powder**

2 stalks diced **celery**

1/2 teaspoon **red pepper flakes**

1 1/4 cups **white rice**, uncooked

2 1/2 cups **chicken broth**

1 teaspoon **salt**

Directions

Slice Andouille sausage into rounds, set aside.

Cut boneless and skinless chicken breasts into 1 inch pieces, set aside.

Season the sliced chicken breasts and sausage with Cajun seasoning, set aside.

In a large Dutch oven, heat ½ of the peanut oil on medium high heat.

Sauté sausages until golden brown, remove from fire, and set aside.

Add ½ of the peanut oil, sauté chicken until lightly brown, remove from fire, and set aside.

In the same pot, sauté garlic, onion, bell pepper and celery in the remaining oil in the same pot.

Add crushed tomatoes. Add black pepper, red pepper, hot pepper sauce, and salt, file powder and Worcestershire sauce, and stir until blended.

Add sautéed sausage and chicken, stir and cook for 10 minutes.

Stir in uncooked rice and chicken broth, stir and bring to a boil.

Simmer Jambalaya over low fire for 20 to 25 minutes, until rice is cooked and liquid is dried.

Enjoy!

Nutritional Information: 465 calories; 19.8 g fat; 42.4 g carbohydrates; 28.1 g protein; 73 mg cholesterol; 1633 mg sodium.

Creole Corn

This Southern-style appetizer will ignite your cravings for something spicy and yummy. It does not only look appealing with its colorful combinations of tomatoes, green and red peppers, and corn, but it can stir your senses.

Servings: 4-6

Ingredients

4 diced **bacon strips**
1 small thinly sliced **onion**
1/4 cup chopped **green pepper**
¼ cup chopped **sweet red pepper**
2 cups chopped seeded **tomatoes**
2 teaspoons **Creole seasoning**
1 to 2 **bay leaves**
2 cups frozen or fresh **corn**
1/4 teaspoon **pepper**

Directions

Cook bacon in a large skillet over medium heat. Remove crisp bacon using a slotted spoon. Drain excess oil on paper towels, reserve oil drippings.

Sauté the peppers and the onion in oil drippings, until they become soft.

Stir in tomatoes and bay leaves, cook without cover on medium low heat for 10 minutes.

Pour corn, cook on low fire uncovered for 10 minutes until corn is soft.

Remove bay leaves and stir in Cajun seasoning. Sprinkle creole with bacon. Enjoy!

Nutritional Information: 874 calories; 41.3 g fat; 105.8 g carbohydrates; 34 g protein; 0 mg cholesterol; 3441 mg sodium.

CREOLE FRIED SNAPPER

Red snapper fish is a joy to eat. Its natural flavor adds your dish a super delicious taste. Fish fillets are more exciting to eat with the perfect blend of herbs and pepper and cooked at high temperature to create a black coating.

Servings: 4

Ingredients

1 1/2 cups melted **butter**

2 teaspoons **garlic powder**

4 pieces (6 ounces) **fillets red snapper**

1 tablespoon **salt**

2 tablespoons **paprika**

1 1/2 tsp. **ground white pepper**

1 1/2 tsp. **ground black pepper**

2 teaspoons **cayenne pepper**

2 teaspoons **onion powder**

1 teaspoon **thyme,** dried

1 teaspoon **oregano,** dried

Directions

Combine cayenne pepper, white pepper, paprika, black pepper, onion powder, salt, thyme, oregano and garlic powder in a small bowl.

Heat a cast iron skillet on high temperature for 10 minutes.

Dip fillet in butter and sprinkle with seasoning evenly on each side.

Place seasoned fillets in the skillet.

Pour about 1 tablespoon of butter on top of each fillet, cook until the underside coating becomes black for 3 to 5 minutes.

Turn fish fillet and pour 1 tablespoon of butter on top and cook for 2 minutes until it becomes flaky.

Enjoy!

Nutritional Information: 806 calories; 5.9 g carbohydrates; 36.4 g protein; 72 g fat; 2312 mg sodium; 245 mg cholesterol

CREOLE FRIED CATFISH

Fried catfish cooked with seafood seasoning, butter, Worcestershire sauce and chili-garlic sauce makes its taste so irresistible. Serve this with Cajun style cooked wild rice.

Servings: 3

Ingredients

2 (4 ounce) fillets of fresh **catfish**

1/2 cup **vegetable oil** for frying

1 package (6 ounces) **long grain, wild rice mix**

1 tablespoon **butter**

1/2 cup diced medium **onion**

1 tablespoon **seafood seasoning**

1 can (15 ounces) crushed **tomatoes**

1 can (6 ounces) tomato paste with **roasted garlic**

1 **egg**

2 1/4 cups **water**

Additional 2 teaspoons **butter**

1/2 cup diced **celery**

1/2 cup diced **green bell pepper**

1 tablespoon of **Worcestershire sauce**

2 teaspoons **chili powder**

2 teaspoons **cornstarch**

3 dashes **chili-garlic sauce**

1/4 cup **quick-mixing flour**

2 tsp. **cayenne pepper**

Salt and **ground black pepper**

1 cup **panko bread crumbs**

Directions

Cut catfish in half crosswise and cut lengthwise into 1 inch wide strips.

In a saucepan, combine 1 tablespoon butter with rice mix with seasoning contents inside the packet, and water and bring to a boil over medium heat.

Lower heat, cover saucepan and simmer until rice is cooked and liquid is absorbed for 25 minutes. Set aside.

In another saucepan, melt 2 teaspoons of butter on medium-low heat.

Stir in celery green bell pepper and onion until tender for 10 minutes.

Add Worcestershire sauce, seafood seasoning, tomatoes, cornstarch, chili powder and tomato paste with garlic, stir until smoothly blended and no more lumps.

Add chili-garlic sauce and simmer, stirring constantly.

Whisk in cayenne pepper, flour, salt and black pepper in a bowl. In a separate bowl, beat egg.

In another bowl, place panko crumbs. Dredge catfish in seasoned flour and remove excess flour by tapping off.

Dip fish in well-beaten egg before dredging in panko crumbs, remove excess crumbs by tapping.

Do this process in another batch of fish.

In a skillet, heat vegetable oil on medium heat, pan-fry fish until golden brown turning each side for 2 minutes.

Place fish on paper towel lined plate to drain excess oil.

Transfer cooked rice to a platter and top with pan-fried seasoned fish pieces.

Pour creole sauce on top of fish and rice edge.

Nutritional Information: 20.2 g fat; 92.2 g carbohydrates; 1666 mg sodium; 616 calories; 28.7 g protein; 117 mg cholesterol

Cajun Fries

The taste of potatoes cooked in Cajun seasoning, and soaked in hot sauce adds a flavorful taste to your fries. Cajun fries are a comfort food that you can never ignore.

Servings: 6

Ingredients

1/4 cup of **olive oil**

1 teaspoon **chili powder**

1 teaspoon **garlic powder**

1 teaspoon **of Cajun seasoning**

1 teaspoon onion powder

6 large **potatoes** for baking

1 teaspoon **sea salt**

Directions

Slice potatoes into thin wedges, set aside.

Preheat oven at 400 degrees F.

In a large resealable bag, combine oil, garlic, chili powder, onion powder, sea salt and Cajun seasoning.

Mix well until ingredients are fully blended. Add sliced potatoes and toss with seasoned oil.

On a baking sheet, arrange potatoes in one layer. Bake potatoes for 35 minutes.

With a spatula, stir potatoes and continue baking until crispy for additional 10 minutes.

Nutritional Information: 9.4 g fat; 0 mg cholesterol; 7.7 g protein; 65.5 g carbohydrates; 399 mg sodium; 369 calories

New Orleans Barbecue Shrimp

Try this shrimp cooked with spice mixture, butter, herbs and Worcestershire sauce. Nothing can beat its excellent taste. This is best served with French bread, pasta and wine.

Servings: 4

Ingredients

1 pound peeled and deveined medium **shrimp**
1/2 cup **butter**
4 cloves minced **garlic**
1 teaspoon **garlic powder**
1/4 cup **beer** (not cold)
1 teaspoon **onion powder**
1/2 teaspoon **dried rosemary**
1/4 teaspoon **cayenne pepper**
1/3 teaspoon **paprika**
1 tablespoon **Worcestershire sauce**
1 teaspoon **dried basil**
1/2 teaspoon **dried thyme**
Salt to taste

Directions

Combine and stir onion powder, garlic powder, thyme, basil, rosemary, paprika and cayenne pepper in a mixing bowl until blended. Set aside.

In a skillet, melt the butter on medium heat. Stir in garlic until aroma comes out for 1 minute.

Stir in shrimp and cook until center turns dark pink. Season shrimp with spice mixture and stir to cook for a few minutes.

Add Worcestershire sauce and beer, stir and simmer for 1 minute.

Add salt according to your taste.

Enjoy!

Nutritional Information: 345 calories; 25.1 g fat; 4.8 g carbohydrates; 23.8 g protein; 234 mg cholesterol; 375 mg sodium.

Po'Boy

Have an enjoyable brunch with this Po'Boy recipe that is prepared with hot sauce and paper-thin crust and crisp New Orleans styled French roll. The shrimp, spices, herbs and vegetables make this Louisiana sandwich super delicious.

Servings: 4

Ingredients

1 1/2 pounds peeled and deveined medium-size **shrimp**
Vegetable oil for frying

1/2 teaspoon freshly **ground black pepper**

1/2 teaspoon **onion powder**

1 teaspoon **garlic powder**

1 teaspoon **cayenne pepper**

2 1/2 teaspoons **kosher salt**

1 teaspoon **paprika**

1/2 teaspoon **dried thyme**

1/2 teaspoon **dried oregano**

1 cup **buttermilk**

1 1/2 cups **all-purpose flour**

1 cup **cornmeal**

4 pieces 8 inch long **French rolls**

Mayonnaise

For toppings:

Shredded lettuce, dill pickles, sliced tomatoes, and pepper

Directions

Split French rolls into horizontal, set aside.

In a mixing bowl, whisk cayenne pepper, paprika, salt, garlic powder, dried thyme, dried oregano, onion powder and ground black pepper. Stir until blended, set aside.

Place shrimp with 2 tablespoons of spice mix in a bowl. Toss to coat shrimp.

Pour buttermilk into a separate medium bowl, set aside.

Whisk cornmeal and flour in another bowl, set aside.

Heat a heavy, wide pot and pour enough oil up to 2 inches deep.

Use a deep-fry thermometer to measure the temperature up to 350 degrees F.

Dip shrimps in buttermilk and coat them with the flour mixture.

Fry each shrimp in the pot until golden brown for 4 minutes each batch. Drain shrimps with paper towel.

Open French rolls and spread with mayonnaise or remoulade. Top Po'Boy with shredded lettuce, sliced pickles and cooked shrimp.

Serve!

Nutritional Information: 658.9 calories; 40.7 g protein; 86.6 g carbohydrate; 17.2 g fat; 253.3 mg cholesterol; 966.7 mg sodium.

Bourbon Chicken

Chicken can be cooked in a variety of ways. The less common recipe is Bourbon Chicken, inspired from one of New Orleans's street, Bourbon. Of course, it's the bourbon that makes the chicken superb!

Servings: 4

Ingredients

2 tablespoons minced **dried onion**
1 teaspoon **ground ginger**
1/2 teaspoon **garlic powder**
4 skinless and boneless **chicken breast halves**
4 ounces **soy sauce**
1/2 cup **brown sugar**
3/8 cup **bourbon**

Directions

In a mixing bowl, combine soy sauce, ginger, sugar, onion flakes, garlic powder and bourbon until well blended, set aside.

Arrange chicken in a 9 x 13 inch baking dish. Pour soy sauce mixture over chicken breasts.

Cover baking dish and marinate overnight in refrigerator.

Preheat oven at 325 degrees F.

Uncover baking dish and bake marinated chicken in oven.

Baste each side frequently for 1 ½ hours or until juice is clear and chicken is golden brown.

Nutritional Information: 313 calories; 29.3 g protein, 31.2 g carbohydrate, 1.5 g fat; 68 mg cholesterol, 1664 mg sodium.

Louisiana Popcorn

Popcorn rice is cooked with the wonders of chicken stock and bay leaf. This quick recipe will only need you half an hour to cook, highly recommended for busy people.

Servings: 4

Ingredients

1 tablespoon **olive oil**
1 small minced **onion**
1 ½ cups **long-grain white rice** or **popcorn rice**
3 cups **chicken stock**
1 **bay leaf**
Pinch of **salt**

Directions

In a medium saucepan, heat oil on moderate heat.

Stir in onion until translucent for 5 minutes.

Stir in popcorn rice for 2 minutes.

Add chicken stock, cover and bring to a boil.

Season with salt and add the bay leaf.

Reduce heat to low and cook popcorn rice for 18 minutes.

Remove saucepan from fire.

Fluff popcorn rice with a fork before serving.

Nutritional Information: 433 calories; 9.3 g protein, 65 g carbohydrate, 15.8 g fat; 0 mg cholesterol, 2451 mg sodium.

Cajun Country Dough

This versatile dough can be used as turnovers and pie crust, even if it is less flaky. People in Louisiana know this old recipe that has been handed from one generation to the Millennials. What makes this interesting is the infusion of the cherry pie filling to come up with so sweet dough.

Servings: 30

Ingredients

3/4 cup softened **unsalted butter**, softened
1 **egg**
1 **egg white** (for egg wash)
4 1/2 cups **all-purpose flour**
2 teaspoons **baking powder**
1 1/3 cups **white sugar**
1/2 cup **milk**
1 can (12.5 ounce) **cherry pie filling**
1 teaspoon **vanilla extract**
1 teaspoon **salt**

Directions

In a mixing bowl, sift altogether dry ingredients and salt. Set aside.

In another bowl, whisk butter and sugar one at a time. Pour vanilla extract and beat mixture until fluffy. Add egg and beat.

Alternately add flour mixture with milk, and beat, but be careful not to over mix so as not to make the dough so sticky and soft.

Cover dough with plastic wrap and chill for 2 hours or more.

Before rolling the dough out, preheat oven at 350 degrees F.

Roll out dough on a lightly floured board. Cut them into three inch squares.

Spoon out 2 teaspoons of the pie filling into the middle of the square and fold to form into a triangle.

Using fork tines pinch the dough seams to press.

Place dough on a greased baking sheet, giving allowance of 2 inches apart.

Brush dough with egg wash before baking for about 12 to 15 minutes until tops and bottom of dough turn golden brown.

Enjoy!

Nutritional Information: 2.5 g protein; 19 mg cholesterol; 119 mg sodium; 162 calories; 5 g fat; 26.8 g carbohydrates

Okra Creole

Okra is a good source of fiber and nutrients to stay healthy. With this appetizer, pretty sure, you will enjoy your meal with much gusto. Frozen okra is available in the market, so you have no reason why you can't prepare this veggie side dish.

Servings: 4

Ingredients

2 tablespoons **olive oil**
1 package (16 ounces) frozen cut **okra**
1 can of (16 ounces) diced **tomatoes in juice**
1/2 large chopped **onion**
2 minced cloves **garlic**
1/2 chopped **green bell pepper**
3/8 teaspoon **dried thyme**
2 tablespoons chopped fresh **parsley**
1/4 teaspoon **cayenne pepper**
Pinch of **Salt**
Dash of **pepper**

Directions

In a large skillet, heat olive oil on medium heat.

Sauté onion and garlic until aroma comes out naturally and onion is translucent.

Stir in green pepper until tender.

Pour tomatoes to the mixture.

Season the mixture with parsley, cayenne, pepper, thyme, and salt. Reduce heat and simmer for 5 minutes.

Stir in okra and pour tomato juice to cover the bottom of the skillet.

Cover and continue cooking for 15 minutes until okra is soft but not mushy.

Serve!

Nutritional Information: 0 mg cholesterol; 184 mg sodium; 133 calories; 7.2 g fat; 14.2 g carbohydrates; 4 g protein;

Conclusion

Thank you so much for downloading this eBook. We at Savour Press hope this book serves as your guide in learning more about the Creole and Cajun recipes that originated in Louisiana, particularly in New Orleans. This book offers you recipes that cover all aspects of NOLA cuisine that are popular in restaurants in various parts of the city. Both types of cuisines have similarity, but they differ in the use of tomato based sauces and tomatoes, which is common in Creole food, while Cajun does not. Well, this is what the book all about.

While writing the book, we have agreed to share the recipes that are quick and easy to prepare and the ingredients are familiar to you. Among the most common ingredients used are garlic, onion, celery, thyme, Cajun seasoning, tomatoes, and shrimp. Whether you are cooking a jambalaya or Cajun shrimp, you find it easy to distinguish that they are the foods served in Louisiana restaurants. As soon as you are familiar with the cooking method and ingredients, you will be able to prepare the dishes quickly without even reading the book.

We hope you will enjoy cooking with these recipes.

Thanks again for your support.

Happy Cooking!

Printed in Great Britain
by Amazon